D0772979

How to Analyze the Works of

SYLVIA PLATH

by Victoria Peterson-Hilleque

ABDO
Publishing Company

Essential Critiques

How to Analyze the Works of

SYLVIA
PLATH

by Victoria Peterson-Hilleque

Content Consultant: William K. Buckley
Professor of English, Editor of *Plath Profiles*,
Indiana University Northwest

Credits

Published by ABDO Publishing Company, PO Box 398166, Minneapolis, MN 55439. Copyright © 2013 by Abdo Consulting Group, Inc. International copyrights reserved in all countries. No part of this book may be reproduced in any form without written permission from the publisher. The Essential Library™ is a trademark and logo of ABDO Publishing Company.

Printed in the United States of America,
North Mankato, Minnesota
052012
092012

Editor: Lauren Coss
Series Designer: Marie Tupy

Library of Congress Cataloging-in-Publication Data
Peterson-Hilleque, Victoria, 1971-
  How to analyze the works of Sylvia Plath / Victoria Peterson-Hilleque.
      p. cm. -- (Essential critiques)
  Includes bibliographical references.
  ISBN 978-1-61783-457-8
  1. Plath, Sylvia--Criticism and interpretation--Juvenile literature. I. Title.
  PS3566.L27Z828 2013
  811'.54--dc23
                                    2012016735

Table of Contents

Chapter

1

Introduction to Critiques

What Is Critical Theory?

What do you usually do when you read a book? You probably absorb the specific language style of the book. You learn about the characters as they are developed through thoughts, dialogue, and other interactions. You may like or dislike a character more than others. You might be drawn in by the plot of the book, eager to find out what happens at the end. Yet these are only a few of many possible ways of understanding and appreciating a book. What if you are interested in delving more deeply? You might want to learn more about the author and how his or her personal background is reflected in the book. Or you might want to examine what the book says about society—how it depicts the roles of

women and minorities, for example. If so, you have entered the realm of critical theory.

Critical theory helps you learn how various works of art, literature, music, theater, film, and other endeavors either support or challenge the way society behaves. Critical theory is the evaluation and interpretation of a work using different philosophies, or schools of thought. Critical theory can be used to understand all types of cultural productions.

There are many different critical theories. If you are analyzing literature, each theory asks you to look at the work from a different perspective. Some theories address social issues, while others focus on the writer's life or the time period in which the book was written or set. For example, the critical theory that asks how an author's life affected the work is called biographical criticism. Other common schools of criticism include historical criticism, feminist criticism, psychological criticism, and New Criticism, which examines a work solely within the context of the work itself.

What Is the Purpose of Critical Theory?

Critical theory can open your mind to new ways of thinking. It can help you evaluate a book from a new perspective, directing your attention to issues and messages you may not otherwise recognize in a work. For example, applying feminist criticism to a book may make you aware of female stereotypes perpetuated in the work. Applying a critical theory to a book helps you learn about the person who created it or the society that enjoyed it. You can also explore how the work is perceived by current cultures.

How Do You Apply Critical Theory?

You conduct a critique when you use a critical theory to examine and question a work. The theory you choose is a lens through which you can view the work, or a springboard for asking questions about the work. Applying a critical theory helps you think critically about the work. You are free to question the work and make an assertion about it. If you choose to examine a book using biographical theory, for example, you want to know how the author's personal background or education inspired or shaped the work. You could explore why the author was drawn to the story. For instance, are there any parallels between a particular character's life and the author's life?

Forming a Thesis

Ask your question and find answers in the work or other related materials. Then you can create a thesis. The thesis is the key point in your critique. It is your argument about the work based on the tenets, or beliefs, of the theory you are using. For example, if you are using biographical theory to ask how the author's life inspired the work, your thesis could be worded as follows: Writer Teng Xiong, raised in refugee camps in

> **How to Make a Thesis Statement**
>
> In a critique, a thesis statement typically appears at the end of the introductory paragraph. It is usually only one sentence long and states the author's main idea.

Southeast Asia, drew upon her experiences to write the novel *No Home for Me*.

Providing Evidence

Once you have formed a thesis, you must provide evidence to support it. Evidence might take the form of examples and quotations from the work itself—such as dialogue from a character. Articles about the book or personal interviews with the author might also support your ideas. You may wish to address what other critics have written about the work. Quotes from these individuals may help support your claim. If you find any quotes or examples that contradict your thesis, you will need to create an argument against them. For instance: Many critics have pointed to the protagonist of *No Home for Me* as a powerless victim of circumstances. However, in the chapter "My Destiny," she is clearly depicted as someone who seeks to shape her own future.

How to Support a Thesis Statement

A critique should include several arguments. Arguments support a thesis claim. An argument is one or two sentences long and is supported by evidence from the work being discussed.

Organize the arguments into paragraphs. These paragraphs make up the body of the critique.

In This Book

In this book, you will read summaries of famous books by writer Sylvia Plath, each followed by a critique. Each critique will use one theory and apply it to one work. Critical thinking sections will give you a chance to consider other theses and questions about the work. Did you agree with the author's application of the theory? What other questions are raised by the thesis and its arguments? You can also find out what other critics think about each particular book. Then, in the You Critique It section in the final pages of this book, you will have an opportunity to create your own critique.

Look for the Guides

Throughout the chapters that analyze the works, thesis statements have been highlighted. The box next to the thesis helps explain what questions are being raised about the work. Supporting arguments have been underlined. The boxes next to the arguments help explain how these points support the thesis. Look for these guides throughout each critique.

Sylvia Plath's deeply personal work has made her one of the best-known writers of the twentieth century.

2

A Closer Look
at Sylvia Plath

Sylvia Plath was born on October 27, 1932, in Boston, Massachusetts, to parents Otto and Aurelia Plath. Otto was a professor at Boston University. Aurelia stayed at home with Sylvia and her younger brother, Warren, who was born in 1935. After Warren's birth, the family moved to Winthrop, Massachusetts, a coastal town near Boston.

Sylvia showed academic talent at a young age, a gift recognized and supported by her parents. However, Otto's dedication to his work and his poor health kept him at a distance from his family. He refused to get medical help, and in November 1940, when Sylvia was eight years old, Otto died from complications related to diabetes, an easily treatable disease at the time. Sylvia would grapple with the loss of her father for the rest of her life. The loss of Otto's salary quickly put the family in dire financial straights. In 1942, the family moved to Wellesley, Massachusetts, where Aurelia barely managed to support Sylvia and Warren by teaching. Aurelia's parents moved in with the struggling family to help.

A Smith Girl

Plath had always been an excellent student. She was particularly gifted at English and creative writing. Her first published poem appeared in the *Boston Herald* in 1941, when she was only eight years old. She started keeping a journal in 1944. In 1950, Plath graduated from high school with honors and attended Smith College in Massachusetts on a scholarship. Often driving herself to the point of illness, Plath excelled at Smith. Her professors considered her to be intelligent, hardworking, and charming. In 1951, she started dating Dick Norton, a senior at Yale University in Connecticut, though the couple never married. Plath continued writing poems and fiction, some of which were published in various journals and magazines. But she also loved creating visual art. She was uncertain about whether she wanted to pursue English or art in her

Plath excelled academically during her time at Smith College in Northampton, Massachusetts.

studies at Smith. As much as possible, she sought to earn money with her writing to relieve the ongoing financial stresses in her family.

In 1953, over the summer following her junior year at Smith, Plath spent a month in New York City as a guest editor of the magazine *Mademoiselle*.

While it was a prestigious internship, Plath received constant criticism from Cyrilly Abels, her mentor at the publication. Upon returning home, Plath learned she had been rejected from attending a creative writing workshop at Harvard University taught by poet Frank O'Hara. Plath began to feel she would never realize her goals as a writer and slipped into a depression. She attempted to seek professional help for her mental health, but the treatment, poorly executed electroshock therapy, only exasperated her depression. On August 24, 1953, Plath left a note saying she was going for a long walk, took a bottle of her mother's sleeping pills, and hid in a crawl space under the porch of her home. She was found near death two days later.

Surviving Suicide

Olive Higgins Prouty, Plath's financial supporter and mentor at Smith, provided the money for several rounds of psychiatric treatment for Plath, and she soon returned to Smith. Already well-known at Smith due to her literary achievements, Plath's widely publicized two-day disappearance and suicide attempt earned her a lot of attention.

Plath did not believe her mental health struggles fueled her creative work. After her suicide attempt she claimed her writing came from her sanest self: "When you are insane, you are busy being insane —all the time. . . . When I was crazy, that was *all* I was."[1]

In 1955, Plath graduated with honors from Smith. That fall, she went on to Newnham College at Cambridge in England to study English on another scholarship. In her journals during this time, Plath expresses conflicting feelings about wanting marriage and a family but also wanting to pursue a career as a writer. Uncertain about whether she could do both, and having few role models from which to learn from, she decided to forge a life as a writer with a family. While at Cambridge, Plath met and began a romance with well-known English poet Ted Hughes. The couple married on June 16, 1956. Shortly after her marriage and 22 months after arriving at Cambridge, Plath wrote in her journal, "And I told myself, coming over, I must find myself: my man and my career: before coming home."[2]

Career and Marriage

The young couple moved to the United States in 1957, where Plath taught at Smith and later worked part time as a secretary. She also typed and promoted Hughes's work. The couple moved back to England in December 1959, where their first child, Frieda, was born in the spring of 1960. That fall, Plath's first book of poems, *The Colossus and Other Poems*, was published. In 1961, Plath began writing a novel, *The Bell Jar*, and gave birth to a second child, Nicholas, in January 1962. Over this period, Plath's work shifted from a controlled academic voice to a more colloquial voice.

In 1962, Plath learned that Hughes had been having an affair. Later that year, the couple separated and Plath and her children moved to London, England. Despite battling depression, she wrote prolifically during this time and seemed to feel a rare confidence about the quality of her work. She wrote *Three Women*, a radio play that was broadcast on BBC radio in August. In January 1963, *The Bell Jar* was published. But Plath's depression worsened, and she sought professional help. She started regularly seeing a therapist and taking antidepressant medication. However, this

treatment did not take effect quickly enough to save Plath's life. On February 11, 1963, after leaving her children bread and mugs of milk and sealing the kitchen to protect them from gas, Plath took a bottle of sleeping pills, turned on the oven gas, and put her head in the oven. She died of gas inhalation.

Plath and poet Ted Hughes honeymooned in Paris, France, after their marriage in 1956.

Plath would never see much of her work published. *Ariel* was published in 1965, two years after her death.

Posthumous Publications

Most of Plath's work was published after her death. *Ariel* was released in 1965. The book contained the poems she was writing at the end of her life, including her now-well-known poems "Lady Lazarus" and "Daddy." Poems Plath did not include in *Ariel* were included in the books *Crossing the Water* and *Winter Trees*, both published in 1971. Plath's mother published her daughter's letters in 1975, in a book titled *Letters Home*. Hughes released a collection of Plath's fiction titled *Johnny Panic and the Bible of Dreams and Other*

Prose Writings in 1977. In 1982, he published Plath's journals. Her poetry collection *Collected Poems*, published in 1981, won the Pulitzer Prize, a prestigious literary award, in 1982. However, there is still missing work by Plath that has never been published, including an incomplete novel and the journals from the end of her life. Hughes said he destroyed Plath's later journals because he feared the contents would distress their children. Plath is buried in the Heptonstall Churchyard in Yorkshire, England.

In 1979, *The Bell Jar* was adapted into a film.

Chapter

3

An Overview of
The Bell Jar

The Bell Jar begins in New York City in the summer of 1953 and closely follows Plath's own experiences during her summer stint as a guest editor at *Mademoiselle* following her junior year at Smith.

Esther Greenwood is working as a guest editor for a fashion magazine. Eleven other young women were also chosen to be guest editors for the summer. Despite Esther's successes as a student at Smith College, she feels insecure about her future. She struggles to understand her place among the other guest editors, unsure of whether she should be a model, rule-abiding young woman or a rule-breaking rebel. Esther is also uncertain about how she wants to spend her life after college. She believes she must choose between having a career and having a family. Esther struggles to keep up with the demands of the guest editor program, including the high expectations of her boss Jay Cee and the pressure to attend the many parties hosted by sponsors of the program. At one such luncheon, hosted by the *Ladies Home Journal*, Esther and the other attending guest editors get food poisoning. Then later, during a photo shoot, Esther admits she wants to be a poet before bursting into tears, revealing the stress she is experiencing. She becomes depressed.

Esther had been seriously dating Buddy Willard at Smith. But Buddy and Esther have grown apart as he recovers from tuberculosis. After learning Buddy had a physical relationship with a waitress over the summer, Esther decides Buddy would not be a good lifetime partner. She decides she wants to expand her own romantic experiences because she does not think men and women should be held to different standards of purity. On the last night of her internship, Esther attends a dance at a country club on a blind date. Her date tries to rape her, though Esther fights him off. After escaping, Esther throws all her clothes off the roof of her hotel. She has to borrow an outfit for the train ride home.

Back at Home

The depression that began in New York worsens when Esther returns home to the suburbs of Boston. She is not looking forward to spending the rest of the summer with her mother and neighbors, including Dodo Conway, a Catholic woman who has six children and is pregnant with a seventh. Esther learns she has been rejected from a summer writing course she had wanted to take and feels defeated and even more depressed. She decides writing is the only thing she wants to study. Mrs. Greenwood tries to teach Esther shorthand

Mademoiselle was a popular magazine in the 1950s. Plath based *The Bell Jar* on her own experiences as a guest editor at *Mademoiselle*.

writing, a skill needed to become a secretary. But Esther does not want to become a secretary and serve men. Eventually, she stops bathing, does not change her clothes, and suffers from insomnia. She finds herself unable to read or write because the letters look distorted to her. Esther's mother helps her seek treatment. Esther sees a psychiatrist, who recommends electroshock therapy. Esther undergoes the therapy and hates it. She refuses to see the psychiatrist for further treatment.

Esther's mental illness worsens, and she decides to kill herself. Contemplating and experimenting with different methods, she tries cutting her legs to see if she could cut her wrists. She also tries hanging and drowning herself unsuccessfully. Finally, she hides in the basement of her mother's home and takes many sleeping pills. Esther is found several days later, barely alive. She is hospitalized with an injury to her cheek and temporary blindness in one eye. After emerging from a coma, Esther receives treatment in the psychiatric ward of a Boston hospital. Esther's mother cannot afford to pay for her treatment, so Esther's scholarship patroness at Smith College, Philomena Guinea, offers to cover the expenses. Now a wealthy successful author, Guinea once had a breakdown of her own and is sympathetic to Esther's needs. Guinea then sends Esther to a private psychiatric facility in the country to treat her mental illness.

At the Hospital

At the new private hospital, Esther has trouble connecting with the other women, but she appreciates Dr. Nolan, the female psychiatrist in charge of her care. Dr. Nolan earns Esther's trust and persuades her to undergo another round of electroshock therapy. Based on her past experiences, Esther is reluctant to undergo the therapy, but Dr. Nolan promises it will not be painful or as traumatic as the first time. The therapy, along with other forms of treatment, helps Esther recover more rapidly. Dr. Nolan also frees Esther from receiving visitors, including Mrs. Greenwood, because she believes the visitors hinder Esther's recovery.

Taking time in the hospital to explore her feelings for Buddy more freely, Esther decides she never loved him. Then, one day, a nurse tells Esther that a new patient knows her. The patient is Joan Gilling, who has just been admitted to the hospital. Not only does Esther know her from Smith, but

Joan also dated Buddy. Esther is upset when she finds Joan in bed with another female patient, not because she is interested in Joan, but because Esther is repulsed by same-sex relationships. Joan tells Esther she likes her better than she liked Buddy.

Esther tells Dr. Nolan about her desire for the romantic freedom that men enjoy and discusses her fears of pregnancy. Dr. Nolan helps her obtain a birth control device, even though it is illegal in Massachusetts at the time. On a temporary leave from the psychiatric hospital, Esther meets a Harvard professor who becomes Esther's first sexual partner. Afterward, Esther is bleeding heavily and the professor drives her to Joan's apartment, as Joan has recently been released from the psychiatric hospital. Esther is still bleeding, and Joan takes her to the hospital. Esther recovers and returns to the psychiatric hospital. Several nights later, Esther learns Joan has committed suicide.

Not long before Esther's discharge from the psychiatric hospital, Buddy comes to visit her, and they discuss the end of their relationship. He wonders aloud if anyone will ever marry her. Although Esther secretly fears the bell jar of insanity may descend on her again in the future, the novel ends with Esther entering her discharge meeting from the psychiatric hospital with the expectation that she will return to Smith College.

Plath, shown in the mid-1950s, based *The Bell Jar* on events from her personal life.

How to Apply Biographical Criticism to *The Bell Jar*

No. 2

What Is Biographical Criticism?

Biographical criticism explores the potential connections between authors and their works. While no work of literature is a perfect replica of real life, looking into an author's life may enrich a reader's understanding of the text.

A biographical critic looks at the personal history of an author and the way it is overtly and covertly reflected in literature by that author. Overt revelations are intended by the author, but covert revelations are unintended by the author. Covert revelations are of special interest to the biographical critic but can be difficult to prove.

Applying Biographical Criticism to *The Bell Jar*

Plath's novel, *The Bell Jar*, was distinctly autobiographical to the point that she published it under the pseudonym Victoria Lucas in fear that the novel might hurt those portrayed in it. The novel overtly reconstructs the period in Plath's life prior to her attempted suicide in her twenties and traces her recovery. The character Esther Greenwood covertly reveals the frustrations Plath was experiencing with her own life as she was writing *The Bell Jar*.

Esther's reaction to Buddy's relationship with the waitress reflects Plath's frustrations with Hughes's infidelity. Jealousy was a factor in Plath's marriage as it was in Esther's relationship with Buddy. Sometimes Plath's jealousy mixed with her depression drove her to commit irrational actions. When Hughes returned home from an

Thesis Statement

This thesis statement argues: "The character Esther Greenwood covertly reveals the frustrations Plath was experiencing with her own life as she was writing *The Bell Jar*." In this essay, the author considers the covert connections between Plath's life and her writing and the way these connections manifest themselves in *The Bell Jar*.

Argument One

The author of this essay has begun to argue her thesis with the first argument: "Esther's reaction to Buddy's relationship with the waitress reflects Plath's frustrations with Hughes's infidelity." The author provides evidence from the text and Plath's biography to make this comparison.

interview late one day, he discovered Plath had destroyed some of the writing he had been working on because she was jealous of the woman who interviewed him. One night she ripped the phone out of the wall, believing Hughes had a suspicious

Daniel Craig and Gwyneth Paltrow starred as Hughes and Plath in the 2003 movie *Sylvia*, based on the romance between the two poets.

conversation. Later, she destroyed both their writings in a bonfire.

Esther is not dating someone she loves deeply, so she does not express jealousy in the same way as Plath did. However, her relationship with Buddy brings out a different kind of jealousy when he tells Esther he had an affair with a waitress. Esther is not jealous of the other woman but of the double standard that allows Buddy to have many romantic encounters while she remains a virgin. She even thinks he gets tuberculosis as a "punishment for living the kind of double life. . . . feeling so superior to people."[1] She determines Buddy would not make a good husband, and she decides to lose her virginity at the earliest opportunity. Esther's reaction to Buddy's infidelity could be seen as a covert reflection of Plath's jealousy over Hughes's infidelity.

Plath reflects on her frustrations about life as a writer and a mother when she creates a character who does not believe she can have both a career and a family. Both Esther and Plath

---

Argument Two

The second argument states: "Plath reflects on her frustrations about life as a writer and a mother when she creates a character who does not believe she can have both a career and a family." This point addresses the fact that the protagonist of *The Bell Jar* rejects the idea that a woman can have the kind of life Plath is living at the time.

are writers. Yet Esther chastises herself, arguing she has nothing to write about because she has limited life experiences. She explains, "How could I write about life when I'd never had a love affair or a baby or even seen anybody die?"[2] Plath had many life experiences prior to writing *The Bell Jar*, but she also expressed concerns about her inability to pursue her life as a writer uninterrupted by outside work such as teaching. In her journals, Plath writes of poetry as being "unlucrative."[3] Yet she also acknowledges her belief that her work as a writer makes her an equal partner in her marriage: "If I can build myself and my work I will be a contribution to our pair, not a dependent and weak half."[4] Plath is forging the kind of life as a wife, mother, and writer that her protagonist in *The Bell Jar* does not believe is possible. Still, Esther's fears reflect the challenges in Plath's life as she writes *The Bell Jar*, suggesting Plath is uncertain she can do all she has set out to do.

Esther's dislike for children illustrates Plath's ambivalence about her decision to become a mother. In addition to recording

> **Argument Three**
> The third argument further examines Esther's and Plath's views on family life by discussing their feelings toward children. The third argument reads: "Esther's dislike for children illustrates Plath's ambivalence about her decision to become a mother."

fights about housework in her journals, Plath writes of concerns about the need for steady income. Esther expresses these same concerns early in the novel when she is considering whether to be a writer or have a family. Esther also expresses a deep loathing for Dodo Conway, who has nearly seven children. When Dodo pushes the youngest child along the sidewalk below Esther's bedroom window, Esther announces: "children made me sick."[5]

While writing *The Bell Jar*, Plath was not only struggling to care for her daughter, Frieda, but she also had a miscarriage and eventually gave birth to Nicholas. Even though she loved her children, she wrote in letters to her mother that it was difficult to manage their care and the household. She was so upset that she told the man who lived in the apartment below hers, who was not a close friend, that she was overwhelmed by the care of her children and home. After her death, Hughes destroyed the journals she wrote while authoring *The Bell Jar* because of the sensitive material they contained, which he did not want their children to see. All of this evidence supports the idea that Esther's loathing of children at times reflected Plath's own feelings.

<u>Esther's struggle with schizophrenia mirrors Plath's own struggles with mental illness.</u> Many professionals in the mental health field have attested to the novel's accurate descriptions of schizophrenia, from which Plath suffered. Esther's mental illness manifests itself in a way very similar to Plath's when she was young, beginning with the guest editor program and worsening after she returns home.

> **Argument Four**
>
> The fourth argument of the essay states: "Esther's struggle with schizophrenia mirrors Plath's own struggles with mental illness." The author explores the way the novel reflects Plath's struggle with mental illness not only as a college student but also during the time she wrote *The Bell Jar*.

Like Plath, Esther's illness drove her to attempt suicide, and like Plath, Esther was found and saved. However, Plath was not just writing from memories of suffering from mental illness when she was young. Her mental illness was an ongoing problem. She began secretly seeing a therapist while living in Boston with Hughes. After moving back to England and following the birth of her two children, Plath continued struggling with mental illness. She did not seek professional help during this time, but friends were concerned about her.

Argument Five

The final argument focuses on Esther's rebirth: "Esther's rebirth at the end of the novel foreshadows the kind of rebirth Plath wants at the end of her marriage." The author develops the concept of rebirth, suggesting Plath's fears about living without her husband mirror her main character's needs after surviving her suicide attempt.

Esther's rebirth at the end of the novel foreshadows the kind of rebirth Plath wants at the end of her marriage. When she leaves the mental hospital, Esther considers herself reborn, saying, "there ought, I thought, to be a ritual for being born twice—patched, retreaded, and approved for the road."[6] By the time *The Bell Jar* was published in England in 1963, Plath had left Hughes after confirming he had been unfaithful. Plath's physical and mental health suffered during this time.

Overall, reviews of *The Bell Jar* were favorable, but Plath was distressed by the lack of comment on what she expressed as Esther's rebirth. This reaction reveals Plath's strong connection to the rebirth of the main character and suggests her own need for rebirth. Plath's frustrations with the lack of attention to Esther's rebirth in the novel also suggest Plath was fearful about her rebirth into a life without a spouse. Her focus on death in her poetry written during this time, such as her final poem, "Edge,"

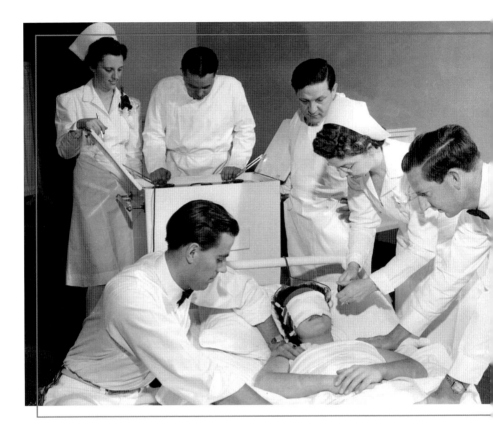

also highlights her inner conflict over how to move forward in her new situation.

Although many overt connections can be found between Plath's life and *The Bell Jar*, several covert connections can also be found between Plath's inner turmoil and Esther's fears and frustrations. While Plath's journals and her biographers provide the evidence needed to understand the complex connections between *The Bell Jar* and Plath's views

Electroshock therapy, which both Plath and Esther underwent, was one technique for treating psychiatric disorders in the 1950s.

Conclusion

This final paragraph is the conclusion of the critique. It sums up the author's arguments and partially restates the original thesis, which has now been argued and supported with evidence from the text. The conclusion also provides the reader with a new idea: that Esther's fears the bell jar would descend again were realized in Plath's life.

on family and career, it would be overreaching to suggest Plath's tragic suicide proves she gave in to the belief that she could not have a career and a family. Her mental illness left her beyond the capacity to make sound decisions. In the end, Esther's fears that the bell jar of madness would descend again were realized in Plath's life.

Thinking Critically about *The Bell Jar*

Now it is your turn to assess the critique. Consider these questions:

1. The thesis argues that Plath's frustrations about her life are reflected in the character Esther Greenwood. Do you agree? Why or why not?

2. What was the most interesting argument made? What was the strongest argument? What was the weakest? Did the arguments support the thesis?

3. The goal of a conclusion is sometimes more than summarizing the argument. A conclusion can also leave the reader with a new, related idea. Do you think this conclusion effectively introduces a new idea? What is it?

Other Approaches

The essay you read is one possible way to apply biographical criticism to a critique of *The Bell Jar*. The following are two alternate approaches for applying biographical criticism to Plath's novel. The first approach compares Plath's relationship with her mother to the character Esther's relationship with her mother. The second approach considers Esther's ideas about purity and romantic relationships with Buddy Willard in light of Plath's relationship with her college boyfriend Dick Norton.

Sympathetic Mothers

Plath writes in her journal of longing for love from her mother but also hating her mother. This complicated relationship can be seen between Esther and her mother in *The Bell Jar*. Esther often portrays her mother negatively. So it is clear to the reader that she does not appreciate her mother. While some argue Esther's and Plath's mothers are unsympathetic, it is also possible to see both mothers as sympathetic figures who love but are unappreciated by their daughters.

A thesis statement comparing the connection between the mothers might be: Esther Greenwood's relationship with her mother is based on Plath's relationship with her mother.

Purity

In *The Bell Jar*, Esther's boyfriend Buddy Willard is thought to be based on Plath's former boyfriend Dick Norton. Plath writes in her journals about Norton seducing a waitress while he was dating Plath, which is something Buddy also did to Esther. Esther was not concerned about the seduction as much as the double standard for men and women. She says,

> It might be nice to be pure and then marry a pure man, but what if he suddenly confessed he wasn't pure after we were married, the way Buddy Willard had? I couldn't stand the idea of a woman having to have a single pure life and a man being able to have a double life, one pure and one not.[7]

The thesis statement for analyzing the relationship between Dick Norton and his fictional counterpoint Buddy Willard might be the following: Plath explored her complicated feelings about Dick Norton through her fictionalization of him as the character Buddy Willard in *The Bell Jar*.

As confessional poetry, Plath's work is intensely personal.

5

An Overview of "Daddy"

Confessional Poetry

Plath is often classified as a confessional poet. Confessional poets are known for heavily using biographical material in their work, often for emotional effect. However, it is important to recognize that the speaker of the poem is not necessarily Plath herself. Plath creates a speaker who, while similar to her, is also different. She may be dealing with emotional truths but not actual realities.

The speaker in "Daddy" explains her father is a German-speaking Polish man whom she could not talk to because she could not speak German and thought the language "obscene."[1] She then compares herself to a person of Jewish descent being sent to a concentration camp during World

War II (1939–1945). The speaker carries the
Holocaust theme over to the descriptions of her
father, focusing on Nazi imagery and saying he has
an Aryan eye. The speaker exclaims, "O you— /
Not God but a swastika."[2] This dark psychological
description of the speaker's inner world is
emphasized when the speaker claims, "Every
woman adores a Fascist / The boot in the face,
the brute / Brute heart of a brute like you."[3] This
imagery explores the complex relationship between
one who has been oppressed and the oppressor.

Rhythm and Rhyme

Initially Plath's poem "Daddy" gives the reader
the impression of entering a nursery rhyme. "You
do not do, you do not do / Any more, black shoe /
In which I have lived like a foot."[4] The use of the
"oo" sound repetitively in the words *you*, *do*, and
shoe gives the speaker of the poem a childlike
voice, especially in conjunction with the content of
the lines.

However, this poem does not have the typical,
orderly four-line stanzas of many nursery rhymes,
nor does it follow predictable rhythm and rhyme
patterns. The five-line stanzas give the poem an

unbalanced feel, as does the uneven syllable count in each line. This gives the reader the sense that the poem is rhythmically teetering, such as in line 15 when the speaker says, "Ach, du."[5] The previous lines were at least twice as long, causing line 15 to stand out in the poem.

It is common for poets using a particular rhythm to break it in order to emphasize a particular phrase or idea. This is especially noticeable when the rhythm is as strong as the one in "Daddy." If rhythms are subtle, then the effects of changes are subtle. If the rhythms are strong, the changes are particularly noticeable. The mesmerizing use of rhythm and sound that Plath establishes in the first stanza changes significantly at line six: "Daddy I've had to kill you. / You died before I had time."[6] The content of this line also alters the tone of the poem. The tone shifts from a playful nursery rhyme to darker imagery where the father is compared to a "bag full of God" and a "ghastly statue."[7] The speaker of the poem indicates her father is dead and she wants to recover him; this complicates the relationship because she also said she wants to kill him.

The twelfth stanza helps clarify the anger and pain expressed previously in the poem when the speaker says she tried to commit suicide after her father died in order to get back to him. The speaker of "Daddy" refers to the death of her father when she was ten years old. Plath may have done this to emphasize that the father died when the speaker was ten, and the speaker tried to kill herself ten years later.

Dark Imagery

It is after the speaker is rescued from her suicide attempt and "stuck" back "together with glue"[8] that she says she made a model of her father: "A man in black with a Meinkampf look."[9] This version of the father is a torturer to whom she said, "I do, I do," indicating marriage.[10] Here, some scholars have made links to Plath's biographical material. Plath explains in her journal that she sometimes identifies Hughes with her father. The link between the speaker and Plath's actual marriage to Hughes is strengthened when the speaker says, "If I've killed one man, I've killed two— / The vampire who said he was you / and drank my blood for a year, / Seven years if you want to know."[11] Plath was married to Hughes for nearly seven years, but the creative distance between the speaker and Plath is clear when she begins speaking of murder and vampires.

Some literary critics believe the reference to "seven years" refers to Plath's seven-year marriage to poet Ted Hughes.

When the imagery of the poem escalates and the speaker compares her father to a vampire whose heart she stakes, it is not clear if she is still referring to the model of her father that she married. It is as if the two men have been merged into one. The poem ends with the image of villagers dancing on the father's grave, and the speaker evokes the strong rhythms running through the poem saying, "Daddy, daddy, you bastard, I'm through."[12]

Plath's poem "Daddy" is rich with imagery and symbolism, making it an interesting choice for a psychoanalytic critique.

6

How to Apply Psychoanalytic Criticism to "Daddy"

No.2

What Is Psychoanalytic Criticism?

A psychoanalytic critic explores literature using the principals of psychoanalysis first developed by Austrian psychologist Sigmund Freud. Freud emphasized the influence the unconscious part of the human mind has on human behavior. He believed the unconscious mind harbored drives such as aggression and sexuality. Freud proposed that humans lack full access to their thoughts. Instead, the ego, or the conscious mind, is frequently at odds with the id, or the unconscious mind, which holds a person's instincts, true desires, and impulses. Because many impulsive feelings cannot be expressed in civilized society, the brain uses the superego, or the conscience, to mediate between the id and the ego. The superego allows some desires through, while repressing, projecting, or distorting others into various symbols or imagery.

Psychoanalytic critics often take Freud's theory and apply it to texts. They look for symbols and imagery in a text that could be tied to repressed material. Because repressed thoughts present themselves indirectly, it can be a challenge to verify claims asserting the meaning of imagery.

Applying Psychoanalytic Criticism to "Daddy"

Rich with haunting imagery and rhythms, Plath's poetry invites the exploration of what the unconscious mind reveals in her text. According to Freud, the unconscious exists in part to store repressed desires and fears that might be uncomfortable. Freud notes that imagery becomes symbolic when it represents something beyond its literal meaning in literature, such imagery can reveal repressed desires and fears indirectly. In the poem "Daddy," the speaker is trying to kill a father who is already dead. The fact that the father in the poem portrays someone who is already dead alerts the reader to the possibility that he is an indirect reflection of repressed emotions. This invites the reader to think of him as a symbol representing something more than just a father. The speaker minimizes her pain over her father's death by distorting her father into various monstrous characters. Transferring her repressed longing for her father into frightening imagery allows some of the speaker's pain to be released.

The ugly imagery about feet and shoes references the speaker's conflicted emotions surrounding her father and her repressed longing for him. These references also point to the transformation of that longing into fear. The speaker begins the poem by comparing herself to a foot living in a black shoe that she cannot bear to live in any longer. The shoe could represent sadness over the loss of the father, which is so painful that the speaker finds it oppressive. She goes on to make many negative

Thesis Statement

The thesis states: "The speaker minimizes her pain over her father's death by distorting her father into various monstrous characters. Transferring her repressed longing for her father into frightening imagery allows some of the speaker's pain to be released." The remainder of the essay discusses how the speaker's unconscious pain is revealed in the poem.

Argument One

The first argument of the essay states: "The ugly imagery about feet and shoes references the speaker's conflicted emotions surrounding her father and her repressed longing for him." This argument shows the ways in which the unconscious can reveal repressed pain and fear by transforming it into imagery.

references to her father's feet and shoes. He is a "Ghastly statue with one gray toe."[1] The speaker also describes her father as a fascist who puts his boot in others' faces. But earlier she confesses, "I never could tell where you put your foot, your root."[2] The foot and boot of the father are linked to the speaker not only because she compared herself to a foot in a boot but also because the root may refer to the father's offspring—the speaker. Her uncertainty about the father's foot and root indicate her own uncertain feelings about her father's death and her relationship to him. Her repressed longing for her father has been so altered by the unconscious that it emerges in symbolic forms representing fear and oppression.

These symbolic forms show up in Holocaust imagery later in the poem. The speaker compares her father to a Nazi, placing herself in the role of a Jewish person. This symbolism indicates the speaker's internal struggle over her inability to connect to her father. Not only does the speaker say she could

---

Argument Two

The second argument of the critique reads: "The speaker compares her father to a Nazi, placing herself in the role of a Jewish person. This symbolism indicates the speaker's internal struggle over her inability to connect to her father." The author argues that the speaker minimizes her repressed longing for her father by imagining him as an oppressive figure.

not speak to her father, but she confuses him with all other Germans saying, "I thought every German was you."[3] Her inability to be close to her father is magnified with references to the Holocaust. Putting the father in the role of monstrous oppressor as a Nazi and herself in the role of victim, the speaker may be able to lessen her sadness over her father's death. Physically the speaker describes her father as completely different from her. He is a powerful "bag full of God" and "big as a Frisco seal."[4] Later, she claims he is "Chuffing me off like a Jew. / A Jew to Dachau, Auschwitz, Belsen."[5] The speaker

Jewish people wait to board a train that will take them to an internment camp during World War II. Plath uses Holocaust imagery throughout "Daddy."

is a gypsy while her father has an "Aryan eye, bright blue."[6] Emphasizing the differences between herself and her father helps relieve some of the pain the speaker has repressed in his absence.

> **Argument Three**
> The third argument states: "The heart imagery also reveals the speaker's repressed longing for her father." The author explains why the speaker relieves some of her pain over the loss of her father when she imagines him biting her heart in two.

The heart imagery also reveals the speaker's repressed longing for her father. Though the speaker seems to hate her father, she also grieves for him. Unable to deal with her complicated emotions, the speaker attempts suicide at age 20 to "get back, back, back to you."[7] The speaker's aim was to be reunited with her father. In this section, she admits to herself her longing to be with him.

She refers to her father as "The black man who / bit my pretty red heart in two."[8] This division implies the speaker's heart was split at her father's death. Imagining that it was a monstrous father who bit her heart in two is less difficult for the speaker than dealing with the pain over his death. This allows the speaker to continue forward as a survivor while relieving some of her repressed anguish over the loss of her father.

After her suicide attempt, the speaker tries an alternative method to deal with her emotions. She creates a model of her father. The dark imagery used in describing this model indicates the speaker's negative feelings toward her father and a need to re-create his presence in her life. She describes this model as "a man in black with a Meinkampf look."[9] This reintroduces the Nazi symbolism from earlier in the poem. Though the speaker desires another version of her father, the new version of Daddy is similarly monstrous to the original. Though she seems to hate her father, she seeks another representation of his oppressive nature. Because her true longing is repressed, the model version of the father is a torturer with "a love of the rack and the screw."[10] Distorting her father releases some of her repressed pain over his death while masking it at the same time.

The speaker also assigns the role of monster to "the vampire who said he was you," symbolizing yet another need for the speaker to recreate the

> **Argument Four**
> The fourth argument further discusses the imagery of the poem: "The dark imagery used in describing this model indicates the speaker's negative feelings toward her father and a need to re-create his presence in her life." This highlights the idea that when the speaker turns her father into a torturer she not only represses her longing for him but also releases it.

role of her father in her life.[11] Again, the speaker places herself in the role of victim, with the vampire drinking her blood. The only way the speaker can break free of this cruelty is to stake the vampire in the heart. This act could symbolize the speaker's rejection of her father's memory. She frees herself from acknowledging her repressed pain over her father's death while actually freeing herself from some of the pain at the same time.

In the poem "Daddy," the speaker distorts her father into monstrous characters to minimize her grief over her father's death. She makes him seem less human and therefore experiences less of a loss. The speaker may also perceive herself as a monster without her father's love. By focusing on murdering her father over and over again, the speaker could be expressing her longing to murder her monstrous existence without him.

Conclusion

This final paragraph is the conclusion of the critique. It sums up the author's arguments and partially restates the original thesis. The conclusion also provides the reader with a new thought—that the father figure in the poem may represent the speaker's own fear that she became a monster after the father's death.

Thinking Critically about "Daddy"

Now it is your turn to assess the critique.
Consider these questions:

1. The thesis argues that in Plath's poem "Daddy" the father actually symbolizes the speaker's repressed longing for her father, which is transformed into a fear of her father. Do you agree? Why or why not?

2. What was the most interesting argument made? What was the strongest one? What was the weakest? Were the points backed up with strong evidence from the work? Did the arguments support the thesis?

3. The goal of a conclusion is sometimes more than summarizing the essay. A conclusion can also leave the reader with a new, related idea. Do you think this conclusion effectively introduces a new idea? What is it?

Other Approaches

There are many other ways to apply psychoanalytic criticism to "Daddy." The previous critique was just one possible example of an essay using Freud's theories. Another essay might focus on Freud's idea of the Oedipal complex. Yet another psychoanalytic critique might further discuss the significance of the Nazi-Jew symbolism in the poem.

The Oedipal Complex

Freud's Oedipal complex explains the way children develop their sense of gender. In Greek mythology, Oedipus unknowingly killed his father and married his mother. Freud argues that boys must learn to identify with the father by relinquishing their desire for their mothers. For girls the opposite holds true: they must learn to relinquish their desire for their fathers and identify with their mothers.

A potential thesis for applying the use of the Oedipal complex to Plath's poem "Daddy" might be: The speaker of "Daddy" unintentionally reveals that her father's untimely death prevented her from relinquishing her repressed desire for her father.

Guilt and the Holocaust

Plath's father died in 1943 during World War II. He was not a soldier and the family was not Jewish. However, it is possible that Plath's references to the Holocaust are an indirect expression of her repressed guilt over the death of her father. It is not uncommon, no matter how unreasonable, for a child to feel responsible for the loss of a parent.

A thesis statement for an essay exploring these ideas could be the following: Plath's repressed feelings of guilt that she may have caused the loss of her father emerge indirectly through her Holocaust imagery in the poem "Daddy."

Like Plath, the speaker of "Lady Lazarus" tries to take her own life multiple times.

An Overview of "Lady Lazarus"

"Lady Lazarus" is a poem about someone who tried to kill herself several times but survives each attempt through the intervention of others. In the poem, the speaker discusses her physical state and her resentment toward being brought back to life and those who rescued her.

A Gruesome Tone

The exultant tone at the beginning of "Lady Lazarus" seems to imply the poem will be a celebration: "I have done it again / One year in every ten / I manage it."[1] The short lines give the poem a fast pace, but the three-line stanzas make it feel a bit unbalanced. This feeling is reinforced in the second stanza when the speaker describes herself as a "walking miracle" with skin as "bright as a Nazi lampshade," a paperweight foot, and a face like a "Jew linen."[2] The reader quickly realizes there is an unsettling edge to the seemingly celebratory tone in the first lines. The speaker goes on to describe herself as something like a corpse, reducing herself to a handful of human parts: skin, a foot, a nose, eye pits, and teeth. This unconventional and grotesque imagery is at odds with the many words that rhyme at the ends of the poem's lines. End rhymes and off rhymes give the poem a formal feeling, such as Plath's use of words such as *again*, *ten*, and *it* in the first stanza. These kinds of rhymes and off rhymes continue throughout the poem. The sense of formality illustrated by the rhyming structure gives the impression the speaker is in full control of her imagery.

Nine Lives

It is unclear whom the speaker is addressing when she says, "O my enemy, / Do I terrify?— / The nose, the eye pits, the full set of teeth?"[3] But she soon shifts her attention from the unnamed enemy to reveal this is not the first time she has nearly died. She compares herself to a cat with nine lives, and she has used three. Her miraculous return to life draws a "peanut-crunching" crowd for whom she performs a "strip tease" with her bandages.[4] While the speaker claims to be the same person as before her near-death experiences, this idea is contradicted by the stark imagery when she describes her corpse-like form.

It is not until midway through the poem that the reader discovers the accomplishment the speaker alluded to in the first line of the poem was the speaker's third attempt at suicide. Her first near-death experience at age ten was not intended. Of her second attempt she says, "I rocked shut / As a seashell. / They had to call and call / And pick worms off me like sticky pearls."[5]

The speaker describes her attraction to death as a call that is easy to follow. She says, "Dying / Is an art, like everything else. / I do it exceptionally well. / I do it so it feels like hell. / I do it so it feels real."[6] What is difficult for the speaker is coming back to life: "To the same place, the same face, the same brute."[7] The speaker seems disgusted by the way others act toward her, as if she is "a miracle."[8] She describes herself as a religious relic saying, "There is a charge / For the eyeing of my scars, there is a charge / For the hearing of my heart—."[9]

Hughes wrote the poem "Last Letter" about the painful emotions surrounding Plath's suicide.

The speaker then further describes the enemies she refers to earlier in the poem. She addresses her doctor in German as "Herr Doktor."[10] Then she calls him her enemy, going on to say, "I am your opus, / I am your valuable, / The pure gold baby / That melts to a shriek."[11] It is not clear who is causing the speaker to burn, the enemy or the speaker herself. However, she is reduced to a pile of ash containing soap, a wedding ring, and a filling. The speaker then rises out of this ash, now addressing her enemies as God and the devil, exclaiming, "Beware / Beware. / Out of the ash / I rise with my red hair/ And I eat men like air."[12]

IN MEMORY
SYLVIA PLATH HUGHES
1932 – 1963
EVEN AMIDST FIERCE FLAMES
THE GOLDEN LOTUS CAN BE PLANTED

People have repeatedly vandalized Plath's grave in Yorkshire, attempting to remove "Hughes" from the gravestone.

8

How to Apply Feminist Criticism to "Lady Lazarus"

No.2

What Is Feminist Criticism?

Feminist criticism is closely associated with the feminist movement of the 1960s and 1970s and is concerned with the way gender inequalities influence and are reflected in texts. Feminist critics consider the gender of the author, the relationships between characters of different genders, and gender relationships during the time the text was produced.

Feminist critics often give voices to women who have been silenced, stereotyped, and simplified in texts. Some critics focus on the ways in which texts by female authors are different from those written by male writers. Others might consider how women are objectified in a text. Feminist critics often focus on the ways a text promotes or undermines ideas about gender during the historical time of the writer, the setting in which the text was written, or the historical time of the critic.

Applying Feminist Criticism to "Lady Lazarus"

The political upheaval signified by women's changing roles in society in the 1960s contrasts starkly with the graduation speech Plath heard at Smith College in 1955. Despite having worked hard to obtain a degree from a prestigious women's college, Smith graduates in 1955 were told that their most important ambition should be to marry. In the 1950s, women had few role models to look to if they wanted to pursue both a career and a family. By the early 1960s, while Plath was balancing life as a wife, mother, and writer, the roles of women had changed significantly. Women were entering the workforce at an increasing rate. However, the traditional stereotypes of a woman as wife and mother subservient to her husband were far from dead. The speaker's descriptions of herself in "Lady Lazarus" reveal her desire to break from the

---

Thesis Statement

The thesis statement in this critique states: "The speaker's descriptions of herself in 'Lady Lazarus' reveal her desire to break from the traditional female stereotype of a woman being defined by her husband." The rest of the essay discusses the ways the speaker rejects being stereotyped as a traditional female.

traditional female stereotype of a woman being defined by her husband.

The speaker emphasizes that she is a "smiling woman," starkly defining female gender in order to undermine it.[1] In the 1950s, while Plath was in college, the expected role for an adult woman was that of a stay-at-home wife and mother. Women were expected to handle housework and care for their husbands and families without complaint. Television shows from this time often portrayed women in exactly this role. However, the traditional image of a 1950s housewife is far from the portrait the speaker offers of herself. The corpse-like description of the speaker just prior to the "smiling woman" line challenges the stereotypical 1950s woman. When the speaker says, "the nose, the eye pits, the full set of teeth," she paints the portrait of a skull.[2] The image of a skull is impressed upon the reader even further with the lines: "Soon the flesh / The grave cave ate will be / At home on me."[3] The speaker has been unable to maintain the pleasant disposition

> **Argument One**
>
> The first argument of the critique states: "The speaker emphasizes that she is a 'smiling woman,' starkly defining female gender in order to undermine it."[4] The author argues that the speaker challenges traditional female stereotypes by comparing herself to a corpse.

Argument Two

The author now shifts the argument to discuss the objectification of the speaker as reflected in the poem's imagery. The second argument states: "The speaker's choice of imagery throughout the poem implies that she sees herself as an objectified woman." The author supports this statement with evidence from the text.

and demeanor expected of a stereotypical woman. Instead, she depicts herself as a rotting corpse.

The speaker's choice of imagery throughout the poem implies that she sees herself as an objectified woman. The speaker compares herself to household objects, including a lamp shade, linen, and a paperweight, illustrating that she sees herself in terms of how she can be of use. This imagery in no way captures the speaker's personality. This form of objectification instead reduces the speaker to the things she does rather than considering her as a whole person. On their own, these images would evoke a housewife whose main purpose is to make life comfortable for her husband. However, the speaker transforms the household objects into grotesque things by identifying them with the Holocaust; she is a "Nazi lampshade" and "Jew linen."[5] Associating household images with the oppression and racism of the Holocaust suggests the speaker finds traditional roles for wives extremely harmful. The references to her attempts at suicide immediately following the household imagery further illustrates the idea that simply being useful to a husband will not provide a woman with a fulfilling life.

As the poem continues, the speaker further emphasizes her own objectification by men. She arranges a striptease, indicating she has allowed this objectification to take place. However, the previous grotesque imagery prevents this striptease from being a case of typical objectification, where the speaker would be identified solely by her sexuality. Since she previously likened herself to a corpse, the speaker has disassociated herself from her own sexuality. As a result, this is an unconventional striptease that allows the speaker to manage her own objectification. She is being watched on her own terms. No longer the stereotypical woman defined by her relationship to her husband, the speaker distances herself further from the traditional female roles that once constrained her.

> **Argument Three**
> The author continues the discussion of objectification with the third argument: "As the poem continues, the speaker further emphasizes her own objectification by men." The author continues discussing the imagery that suggests the men's objectification of the speaker.

However, the speaker has not yet entirely broken free from her female role. The men who bring her back to life think of her as an "opus" and a "pure gold baby."[6] This imagery indicates they treasure her in terms of her physical qualities, rather than her inner worth. An opus, while beautiful, hardly reflects the complexity of a human person any more than a silent, stationary statue made of precious metal. Refusing to let herself be limited by such definitions from men, the speaker rejects this representation of herself and what it means to be female when she "melts to a shriek."[7] She would rather be a pile of ash than limited to traditional female roles defined by a patriarchal society.

After the speaker rises from the ashes, she leaves behind a cake of soap, a wedding ring, and a gold filling. These physical objects could be seen as representing her marriage, indicating the speaker's role as wife is not a part of her rebirth. The imagery of rising from the ashes plays into the legend of the phoenix. This mythical creature was said

> **Argument Four**
>
> The third argument reads: "These physical objects could be seen as representing her marriage, indicating the speaker's role as wife is not a part of her rebirth." The author argues that by leaving behind her traditional female roles, the speaker is free to exact her revenge on her oppressors.

to burst into flames every 500 years. Then it was born again from its own ashes to live a new life. The imagery of the speaker rising from the ashes, in this case being revived after her third suicide attempt, suggests the speaker's rejection of the stereotypical female role in a patriarchal society. The items she leaves behind, including her wedding ring, show that after being reborn, the speaker has left her role of wife behind. Refusing the role assigned her, she abandons everything that could prevent her transformation into a complete person. Unrestricted by the patriarchal ideas about what it means to be

The narrator references the mythical phoenix, which can be found in the legends of different cultures around the world.

a married female, the speaker exacts revenge on males. Her last words are terrifying: "Out of the Ash / I rise with my red hair / And I eat men like air."[8] Those who had objectified the speaker in her past life are now her prey.

Through her descriptions of herself and the imagery in the poem, the speaker in "Lady Lazarus" undermines and rejects the role of the stereotypical 1950s woman. The speaker defies her own classification as a wife by distorting any attempt to associate herself with household objects or a sexual fantasy. The speaker manages to transcend her gender role to live a life outside the stereotypical role of a married woman. Rising from her own ashes, this phoenix-like speaker feeds on the men who brought her back to life. In a reversal of her initial role in the patriarchal society, the speaker is now in control of the men.

Conclusion
This final paragraph is the conclusion of the critique. It sums up the author's arguments and partially restates the original thesis, which has now been argued and supported with evidence from the text.

Thinking Critically about "Lady Lazarus"

Now it is your turn to assess the critique. Consider these questions:

1. The thesis argues that Plath's poem "Lady Lazarus" reflects the speaker's longing to free herself from traditional female stereotypes. Do you agree? Why or why not?

2. Can you think of any other imagery or other evidence from the poem that supports this thesis? Can you think of any evidence that disproves the thesis? Why?

3. Do you agree with the author's statement in the conclusion that the speaker is now in control of the men? Why or why not?

Other Approaches

The essay you read is one possible way to apply feminist criticism to "Lady Lazarus." There are many other ways you could approach the work. Analyzing a work using feminist criticism looks at the way gender relationships affect a work. Following are two alternate approaches. The first approach examines how Plath reinvents mythology about the phoenix to explore feminist issues. The second approach explores the ways the speaker of "Lady Lazarus" is punished for refusing to act according to conventional notions of femininity.

Female Phoenix

Mythology about the phoenix is found in many cultures, and many different stories about the phoenix could be considered alongside the views of feminist critics. One feminist scholar writes,

> *In returning to the ancient myths and opening them from within to the woman's body, the woman's mind, and the woman's voice, contemporary women have felt like thieves of the language staging a raid on the treasured icons of a tradition that has required woman's silence for centuries.*[9]

A feminist critique of "Lady Lazarus" that explores Plath's use of phoenix mythology might use the following thesis statement: Plath creates a new female voice that overcomes oppression from men when she transforms traditional mythology of the phoenix in her poem "Lady Lazarus."

Performing a Lady

Feminist critic Judith Butler strives to distinguish the difference between gender and sex. Being a male or a female is a biological categorization. But being feminine or masculine is a cultural categorization. The characteristics that constitute something as masculine or feminine are defined differently by different cultures. Butler claims gender is constructed and performed by individuals whether they realize it or not and "those who fail to do their gender right are regularly punished."[10]

A thesis for a critique of "Lady Lazarus" that explores the way the speaker is punished for her failure to perform gender according to cultural expectations could read as follows: The speaker of "Lady Lazarus" is punished by the men in her life for not performing her femininity according to cultural norms.

Plath's relationship with Hughes is reflected in much of her work.

An Overview
of *Three Women*

Three Women is a long poem written as a play for the radio. It was first performed on the British Broadcasting Corporation (BBC) in the spring of 1962. The play takes place in a maternity ward. There is no dialogue between the characters of the play, only the alternating voices of three women. The first voice, often referred to as the Wife, gives birth to a healthy baby. The second voice, often referred to as the Secretary, has a miscarriage. The third voice, often referred to as the Girl, gives her baby up for adoption. The Wife and the Secretary both have many more lines than the Girl.

The Wife

The Wife's voice opens the play. She is patient and mentally prepared to give birth and become a mother. Initially, her monologues focus on the process of pregnancy. She believes it comes naturally to her as a woman; she has to put little thought into it: "What happens in me will happen without attention."[1] However, in the hospital as the time of her labor draws closer, the Wife becomes anxious about the waiting and the imminent birthing process: "When will it be, the second when Time breaks / And eternity engulfs it, and I drown utterly."[2] Later, she describes the pain of labor: "There is no miracle more cruel than this. / I am dragged by the horses."[3] She reflects on the brutality of childbirth as well as on the larger implications of parenting. She wonders how such pain could ever produce anything good when she says, "what pains, what sorrow must I be mothering."[4] Eventually, the Wife gives birth to a healthy baby. At first, she remarks on the strangeness of her new son. But as soon as she holds him, the pain of her labor seems to be forgotten:

> What did my fingers do before they held
> him? What did my heart do with this love? /
> I have never seen a thing so clear. / His lids
> are like the lilac-flower / And soft as a moth,
> his breath.[5]

Her desire to protect her infant is contrasted with her concern that she will not be strong enough. She finds reassurance in the natural world. She pushes any fears of abnormal infants from her mind as she begins her life with her son saying, "I shall meditate on normality."[6] She wants him to be ordinary and to love her as much as she loves him.

The Secretary

The Secretary's monologues are of a very different tone than the Wife's. They are filled with grief over the loss of her baby. When she realizes she is miscarrying, she reflects on how the men at her office were unsympathetic to her situation. She describes them as "flat."[7] As she miscarries the child she says, "I am dying as I sit. I lose a dimension."[8] She compares her loss to a disease, death, and even sin. Her sense of loss is heightened when she goes to the hospital to recover, where many of the women around her are in labor or have just given birth to their babies. She says that children "have too many colors, too much life. They are not quiet, / Quiet, like the emptiness I carry."[9]

The Secretary claims she did everything she could to protect her pregnancy and avoid the miscarriage. She is haunted by images of the child that did not survive and almost seems to envy it, calling the child "perfect / In its easy peace."[10] The men who work in her office seem insensitive to her suffering. The Secretary believes they are jealous of her ability to conceive. Ultimately, however, she blames and hates herself for her miscarriage. She compares the earth to a vampire who is kind except to men that use her cruelly. The Secretary also compares the terrible emptiness she feels to a winter that fills her and contrasts sharply with the pregnant women around her.

Preparing to leave the hospital, the Secretary is surprised she does not look as deformed on the outside as she feels inside. The doctors and nurses describe miscarriage as usual and say it happens in 20 percent of pregnancies. Putting on her lipstick, the Secretary feels as if she puts on her old self again. She tries to focus on the positive aspects of her life, such as her work and her husband whom she loves. Still, she argues, "I am flat and virginal, which means nothing has happened."[11] Later, at home, she says she waits and aches. She speaks the last lines of the play, which are hopeful. They focus on green grass coming through stone, as if symbolizing a new beginning that might emerge from loss.

The Girl

Unlike the Wife and the Secretary, the Girl describes herself as not ready to be a mother and intends to give up her baby for adoption. From the beginning, she does not imagine her baby as her own: "The face in the pool was beautiful, but not mine."[12] In her monologues, the Girl frequently refers to hooks, which seem to represent the different responsibilities that haunt her. She says the baby's cries are "hooks that catch and grate like cats."[13] As the Girl leaves the hospital, she describes herself as a "wound that they are letting go."[14] Although she always planned to give the child up for adoption, the Girl struggles with her decision. But in the end, she leaves the baby girl to be adopted: "I leave my health behind. I leave someone / Who would adhere to me: I undo her fingers like bandages: I go."[15] She returns to her life as a student and speaks of healing, but she dreams of her child. She has been changed, though she picks up her old life where it left off. Her final words of the play are, "What is it I miss?"[16]

Plath is shown with her mother, Aurelia, and her two children.

How to Apply Structuralism to *Three Women*

No.2

What Is Structuralism?

Structuralist literary theory was first developed
in France in the 1950s. Swiss linguist Ferdinand
de Saussure deeply influenced early thinkers in
the movement. Structuralist literary critics focus
on the ways language is used to create meaning.
Critics applying structuralism also look for
meaning in the text by considering its relationship
to larger structures the text is a part of, such as a
literary genre. Literary theorist Peter Barry says of
structuralism, "its essence is the belief that things
cannot be understood in isolation—they have to be
seen in the context of the larger structures they are a
part of."[1]

Structuralist critics sometimes look for the way
meaning is created through dyads, word pairs that

are opposites, such as good versus evil, love versus hate, or life versus death. They often propose that one word in the dyad will dominate the other one in a particular text.

Applying Structuralism to *Three Women*

The imagery tied to certain repeating words in *Three Women* calls special attention to those words and the ideas they represent. The speakers in the play often refer to things as being flat or full, which highlights the tension between these two oppositional concepts. The domination of *full* in the dyad flat versus full illustrates the Secretary's grief over her miscarriage.

Flat things in the play are associated with sterility, the business world, and maleness. The Secretary takes an active role in the male world. She works in an office where she is surrounded by men who cannot relate to her situation as

---

Thesis Statement

The thesis statement in this critique asserts: "The domination of *full* in the dyad flat versus full illustrates the Secretary's grief over her miscarriage." The author discusses the way the concepts of fullness and flatness contribute to the play's themes about motherhood.

Argument One

The first argument of the critique states: "Flat things in the play are associated with sterility, the business world, and maleness." The author details the Secretary's experiences with the men in her office.

---

a woman who has recently miscarried. She says the men represent "that flat, flat, flatness from which ideas, destructions, / Bulldozers, guillotines, white chambers of shrieks proceed."[2] Not only is flatness associated with men and business but also machines and destruction. She describes the men as flat "like cardboard, and now I had caught it."[3] The Secretary believes she has taken on these male qualities of flatness. She even seems to blame her miscarriage on this male flatness.

While flat things are associated with maleness, full things are associated with pregnancy, fertility, and femaleness. In her grief over her miscarriage, the Secretary acknowledges she is neither flat nor full. In the maternity ward, the Secretary refers to the pregnant women around her as "mounded."[4] She envies the other women at the hospital. She hears the babies crying and reflects that she carries only silence. Through the birth process, the mountainous state of pregnancy is replaced with the fullness of nourishing a new life.

> **Argument Two**
> The author takes the first argument a step further with the second argument: "While flat things are associated with maleness, full things are associated with pregnancy, fertility, and femaleness." The author highlights different examples of flatness that reflect the Secretary's mourning of the child she lost.

The flatness the Secretary feels after miscarrying her baby is overwhelmed by the presence of pregnant women. Fullness dominates while at the same time highlighting the Secretary's loss.

The Secretary has lost her identity as a woman, relating more to the destructive men. She sees herself as a force of destruction due to her inability to birth her child, saying,

> I see myself as a shadow, neither a man nor woman, / Neither a woman, happy to be like a man, nor a man / Blunt and flat enough to feel no lack. I feel a lack.[5]

Caught in a world between flatness and fullness, the Secretary has lost her identity.

In acknowledging her past fullness, the Secretary recognizes her need to be full again. The Secretary believes men want everything to be flat because they envy things that are not flat. This suggests the superiority of fullness. The Secretary's references to fullness reflect her recognition of this superiority. She says the earth, a round, full object,

---

Argument Three

The third argument states: "In acknowledging her past fullness, the Secretary recognizes her need to be full again." This final argument addresses the fact that pregnancy is a part of a natural cycle of life, and there is hope the Secretary will become pregnant again.

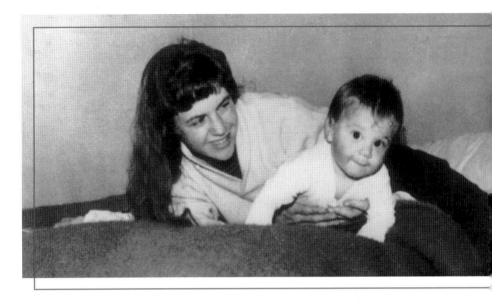

"is the vampire of us all. So she supports us, / Fattens us, is kind."[6] A vampire feeds and grows full off human blood, but this vampire cares for humans and is kind. Comparing the earth to a vampire exemplifies the kind of fullness that dominates in the midst of the Secretary's loss. Without the earth, no life would be sustained. While the Secretary may blame the earth for her miscarriage, she also recognizes the possibility that the earth will provide her with a new child. She may become pregnant again. She leaves the hospital undeformed. When she looks in the mirror, she sees a woman, indicating she is no longer the victim of male flatness. Her last words in the play are ones of hope.

Although Plath gave birth to two healthy children, she suffered a miscarriage before her son, Nicholas, was born.

Conclusion

The final paragraph is the conclusion of the critique. It sums up the author's arguments and partially restates the original thesis. The conclusion also provides the reader with a new thought: the last image of the play is a hard stone being filled with new life, suggesting the Secretary can be filled with new life too.

While at first it may seem as if flatness will dominate over fullness in the dyad flat versus full, it is fullness that ultimately dominates in the oppositional pair. The Secretary uses this dyad to illustrate her grief over her miscarriage. She experiences healing with time. She says, "I find myself again. I am no shadow," suggesting that fullness is slowly coming upon her.[7] This is also reinforced by the last image of the play: "Little grasses crack through stone, and they are green with life."[8] Even a hard stone can be filled with new life; therefore, the Secretary, too, can be full again.

Thinking Critically About *Three Women*

Now it is your turn to assess the critique. Consider these questions:

1. The thesis argues that images of fullness dominate over images of flatness in the play *Three Women*. Do you agree? Why or why not?

2. This critique focuses on the Secretary. Does the dyad flat versus full have significance with the other characters in the play? In what way?

3. In the conclusion, the author suggests the Secretary is becoming full again. Do you agree? Why or why not?

Other Approaches

The essay you read is one way to apply structuralism to a critique of *Three Women*. But there are other ways you could approach it. Analyzing a work using structuralism sometimes looks at the ways oppositional language affects a work. One approach to applying structuralism to *Three Women* could examine an oppositional pairing of two characters—the Wife and the Girl. Yet another approach might explore how the Girl's limited lines affect her role in the play.

Ready or Not?

In the play, the Wife speaks of being ready to be a mother. The Girl says she is not ready, so she gives up her child for adoption. However, the Girl experiences a deep sense of loss after giving up her baby.

A thesis statement for a structuralist critique exploring the meaning of the struggle between being ready and not being prepared for motherhood might be the following: The Wife's readiness and the Girl's unpreparedness for motherhood and their responses following their respective childbirths support the idea that mothering is an instinctual part of being a woman.

The Fear of Deformity

The Girl provides the perspective of one who has held her child, then given up that child. While the other women reclaim their earlier selves by the end of the play, the Girl never returns to the way she was before childbirth. She is the only one without a husband to support her, and she has the least number of lines in the play.

A thesis statement for a structuralist critique considering these ideas might be the following: The Girl's minimal lines when compared to the Wife and the Secretary reflect the struggles of a pregnant, unmarried woman in the 1950s.

You Critique It

Now that you have learned about different critical theories and how to apply them to literature, are you ready to perform your own critique? You have read that this type of evaluation can help you look at literature in a new way and make you pay attention to certain issues you may not have otherwise recognized. So, why not use one of the critical theories profiled in this book to consider a fresh take on your favorite book?

First, choose a theory and the book you want to analyze. Remember that the theory is a springboard for asking questions about the work.

Next, write a specific question that relates to the theory you have selected. Then you can form your thesis, which should provide the answer to that question. Your thesis is the most important part of your critique and offers an argument about the work based on the tenets, or beliefs, of the theory you are applying. Recall that the thesis statement typically appears at the very end of the introductory paragraph of your essay. It is usually only one sentence long.

After you have written your thesis, find evidence to back it up. Good places to start are in the work itself or in journals or articles that discuss what other people have said about it. Since you are critiquing a book, you may also want to read about the author's life so you can get a sense of what factors may have affected the creative process. This can be especially useful if working within historical, biographical, or psychological criticism.

Depending on which theory you are applying, you can often find evidence in the book's language, plot, or character development. You should also explore parts of the book that seem to disprove your thesis and create an argument against them. As you do this, you might want to address what other critics have written about the book. Their quotes may help support your claim.

Before you start analyzing a work, think about the different arguments made in this book. Reflect on how evidence supporting the thesis was presented. Did you find that some of the techniques used to back up the arguments were more convincing than others? Try these methods as you prove your thesis in your own critique.

When you are finished writing your critique, read it over carefully. Is your thesis statement understandable? Do the supporting arguments flow logically, with the topic of each paragraph clearly stated? Can you add any information that would present your readers with a stronger argument in favor of your thesis? Were you able to use quotes from the book, as well as from other critics, to enhance your ideas?

Did you see the work in a new light?

Timeline

1932 Sylvia Plath is born on October 27.

1940 Sylvia's father, Otto Plath, dies in November.

1960 Plath and Hughes's daughter, Frieda, is born in April; Plath publishes *The Colossus and Other Poems* in October.

1961 Plath begins writing *The Bell Jar*.

1962 Plath and Hughes's son, Nicholas, is born in January; Plath separates from Hughes after learning he has had an affair; BBC radio broadcasts *Three Women*.

1963 In January, Plath publishes *The Bell Jar*; Plath commits suicide on February 11.

1950 Sylvia graduates from high school; she begins studying at Smith College in September.

1953 In June, Plath guest edits for one month at *Mademoiselle* in New York City; on August 24, Plath attempts suicide but is rescued.

1955 Plath graduates from Smith; in the fall, she begins studying at Newnham College of Cambridge University.

1956 Plath marries poet Ted Hughes on June 16.

1957 Plath and Hughes move to the United States.

1959 Plath and Hughes move back to England.

Glossary

bell jar
A glass vessel used in laboratories to contain a vacuum.

colloquial
Conversational.

imagery
Comparisons, descriptions, and figures of speech that help the mind form forceful or beautiful pictures.

monologue
A scene or part of a play in which a single person speaks alone.

objectify
To think about someone as an object without considering his or her humanity or personality.

off rhyme
A partial rhyme where words sound similar but are not as closely linked as a true rhyme, such as *root* and *look*.

opus

A musical composition or set of compositions.

patriarchal

Governed and controlled by men.

prolific

Extremely inventive and productive.

protagonist

The main character in a story or poem.

repress

The process of preventing the expression of particular desires.

subservient

Submissive to someone.

symbolism

When images in literature represent something more than their physical attributes.

Bibliography of Works and Criticism

Important Works

The Colossus and Other Poems, 1960

The Bell Jar, 1963

Ariel, 1965

Crossing the Water, 1971

Winter Trees, 1971

Letters Home, 1975

The Bed Book, 1976

Johnny Panic and the Bible of Dreams and Other Prose Writings, 1977

Collected Poems, 1981

The It-Doesn't-Matter Suit, 1996

Mrs. Cherry's Kitchen, 2001

Critical Discussions

Barry, Peter. *Beginning Theory: An Introduction to Literary and Cultural Theory*. New York: Manchester UP, 2002. Print.

Brain, Tracy. *The Other Sylvia Plath*. Harlow, England: Pearson, 2001. Print.

Bundtzen, Lynda K. *Plath's Incarnations: Woman and the Creative Process*. Ann Arbor: Michigan UP, 1983. Print.

Lane, Gary. *Sylvia Plath: New Views on the Poetry*. Baltimore: John Hopkins UP, 1979. Print.

Wagner-Martin, Linda. *The Bell Jar: A Novel of the Fifties*. New York: Twayne, 1992. Print.

Resources

Selected Bibliography

Alexander, Paul. *Rough Magic: A Biography of Sylvia Plath*. New York: Viking, 1991. Print.

Butscher, Edward. *Sylvia Plath: The Woman and the Work*. New York: Dodd, Mead, and Co., 1977. Print.

Kukil, Karen, ed. *The Unabridged Journals of Sylvia Plath*. New York: Anchor, 2000. Print.

Rose, Jacqueline. *The Haunting of Sylvia Plath*. Cambridge, MA: Harvard UP, 1992. Print.

Van Dyne, Susan. *Revising Life: Sylvia Plath's Ariel Poems*. Chapel Hill, NC: North Carolina UP, 1993. Print.

Further Readings

Hemphill, Stephanie. *Your Own, Sylvia: A Verse Portrait of Sylvia Plath*. New York: Knopf, 2007. Print.

Kirk, Connie Ann. *Sylvia Plath: A Biography*. Westport, CT: Greenwood, 2004. Print.

Levy, Pat. *A Guide to the Poems of Sylvia Plath*. London: Hodder and Stoughton, 1999. Print.

Wisker, Gina. *Sylvia Plath: A Beginner's Guide*. London: Hodder and Stoughton, 2001. Print.

Web Links

To learn more about critiquing the works of Sylvia Plath, visit ABDO Publishing Company online at **www.abdopublishing.com**. Web sites about the works of Sylvia Plath are featured on our Book Links page. These links are routinely monitored and updated to provide the most current information available.

For More Information

Plath Profiles

www.iun.edu/~nwadmin/plath

Indiana University Northwest publishes a journal featuring both creative and academic writings based on and inspired by Plath's work.

Smith College

Northampton, MA 01063

413-584-2700

www.smith.edu/newssmith/winter2004/plath.php

Smith College has an extensive collection of Sylvia Plath's papers, including drafts of poems and letters.

Source Notes

Chapter 1. Introduction to Critiques
None.

Chapter 2. A Closer Look at Sylvia Plath
 1. Linda Wagner-Martin. *The Bell Jar: A Novel of the Fifties*. New York: Twayne Publishers, 1992. Print.
 2. Ted Hughes and Frances McCullough, eds. *The Journals of Sylvia Plath*. New York: Ballantine, 1982. 8th ed. 1991. Print. 153.

Chapter 3. An Overview of *The Bell Jar*
None.

Chapter 4. How to Apply Biographical Criticism to *The Bell Jar*
 1. Sylvia Plath. *The Bell Jar*. New York: HarperPerennial, 1999. Print. 73.
 2. Ibid. 112.
 3. Karen Kukil, ed. *The Unabridged Journals of Sylvia Plath*. New York: Anchor Books, 2000. Print. 446.
 4. Ibid. 446.
 5. Sylvia Plath. *The Bell Jar*. New York: HarperPerennial, 1999. Print. 117.
 6. Ibid. 244.
 7. Ibid. 81.

Chapter 5. An Overview of "Daddy"

1. Sylvia Plath. "Daddy." *Collected Poems*. Ed. Ted Hughes. 1981. New York: HarperPerennial, 1992. 222–224. Print. Line 30.
2. Ibid. Lines 45–46.
3. Ibid. Lines 48–50.
4. Ibid. Lines 1–3.
5. Ibid. Line 15.
6. Ibid. Lines 6–7.
7. Ibid. Lines 8–9.
8. Ibid. Line 62.
9. Ibid. Line 65.
10. Ibid. Line 67.
11. Ibid. Lines 15–18.
12. Ibid. Line 80.

Chapter 6. How to Apply Psychoanalytic Criticism to "Daddy"

1. Sylvia Plath. "Daddy." *Collected Poems*. Ed. Ted Hughes. 1981. New York: HarperPerennial, 1992. 222–224. Print. Line 9.
2. Ibid. Lines 22–23.
3. Ibid. Line 29.
4. Ibid. Lines 8–10.
5. Ibid. Lines 32–33.
6. Ibid. Line 44.
7. Ibid. Line 65.
8. Ibid. Lines 55–56.
9. Ibid. Line 59.
10. Ibid. Line 66.
11. Ibid. Line 16.

Source Notes Continued

Chapter 7. An Overview of "Lady Lazarus"
1. Sylvia Plath. "Lady Lazarus." *Collected Poems*. Ed. Ted Hughes. 1981. New York: HarperPerennial, 1992. 244–246. Print. Line 1.
2. Ibid. Lines 4, 5, 8.
3. Ibid. Lines 11–13.
4. Ibid. Line 29.
5. Ibid. Lines 39–42.
6. Ibid. Lines 43–47.
7. Ibid. Line 53.
8. Ibid. Line 55.
9. Ibid. Lines 57–59.
10. Ibid. Line 65.
11. Ibid. Lines 67–70.
12. Ibid. Lines 80–84.

Chapter 8. How to Apply Feminist Criticism to "Lady Lazarus"
1. Sylvia Plath. "Lady Lazarus." *Collected Poems*. Ed. Ted Hughes. 1981. New York: HarperPerennial, 1992. 244–246. Print. Line 19.
2. Ibid. Line 13.
3. Ibid. Lines 16–18.
4. Ibid. Line 19.
5. Ibid. Lines 7, 9.
6. Ibid. Lines 67–69.
7. Ibid. Line 70.
8. Ibid. Lines 82–84.
9. Julie Rivkin and Michael Ryan, eds. *Literary Theory: An Anthology*. 2nd ed. Malden, MA: Blackwell, 2004. Print. 613.
10. W. B. Worthen. *Modern Drama: Plays / Criticism / Theory*. Fort Worth, TX: Harcourt Brace, 1995. Print. 1099.

Chapter 9. An Overview of *Three Women*

1. Sylvia Plath. *Three Women. Collected Poems*. Ed.
Ted Hughes. 1981. New York: HarperPerennial, 1992.
176–187. Print. Line 10.
2. Ibid. Lines 104–105.
3. Ibid. Lines 127–128.
4. Ibid. Line 133.
5. Ibid. Lines 169–173.
6. Ibid. Line 323.
7. Ibid. Line 15.
8. Ibid. Line 30.
9. Ibid. Lines 69–70.
10. Ibid. Lines 88–89.
11. Ibid. Line 276.
12. Ibid. Line 45.
13. Ibid. Line 207.
14. Ibid. Line 271.
15. Ibid. Lines 272–273.
16. Ibid. Line 350.

Chapter 10. How to Apply Structuralism to *Three Women*

1. Peter Barry. *Beginning Theory: An Introduction to Literary and Cultural Theory*. Manchester, UK: Manchester UP, 2002. Print. 39.
2. Sylvia Plath. *Three Women. Collected Poems*. Ed.
Ted Hughes. 1981. New York: HarperPerennial, 1992.
176–187. Print. Lines 18–19.
3. Ibid. Line 17.
4. Ibid. Line 180.
5. Ibid. Lines 190–192.
6. Ibid. Lines 154–155.
7. Ibid. Line 167.
8. Ibid. Lines 369–370.

Index

About the Author

Victoria Peterson-Hilleque is a freelance writer who lives and works in Minneapolis, Minnesota. Her books *How to Analyze the Works of J. K. Rowling* (2011) and *J. K. Rowling a Biography* (2010) were published by ABDO Publishing Company. She has a master's degree in English Literature from the University of St. Thomas and a master's degree in fine arts from Hamline University.

Photo Credits

CSU Archives/Everett Collection, cover, 3, 12, 19, 30, 80, 86, 98 (top); Lana Sundman/Alamy, 15; Jeff Morgan 14/Alamy, 20; AVCO Embassy Pictures/Everett Collection, 22; Archive Photos/Getty Images, 25; David Appleby/Focus Features/ Photofest, 33; AP Images, 39; Everett Collection, 44, 98 (bottom); Leonard Brown/AP Images, 49; Bettmann/Corbis/AP Images, 50; Roger Viollet/Getty Images, 55; Amy T. Zielinski/ Getty Images, 62; Ted Hughes Estate British Library Board/ AP Images, 66; V. Dorosz/Alamy, 68, 99; JinYoung Lee/ iStockphoto, 75; Associated Newspapers/Rex/Rex USA, 91